For my parents and my wife Claudia

LEONARD BERNSTEIN
The Last 10 Years

LEONARD BERNSTEIN

The Last 10 Years
A Personal Portrait by Thomas R. Seiler

With introductory remarks by Hildegard Behrens
and Thomas Hampson and reminiscences of friends,
associates and colleagues

*E*DITION *S*TEMMLE

Zurich New York

... It shows my father as I very much like to remember him: actively in thought ...

Alexander Bernstein

These photographs reveal the true Lenny—the most deeply, touchingly, genuinely, remorsefully theatrical character in music.

In admiration
Yehudi Menuhin

Looking at these marvelous photographs, I find myself filled with many, often conflicting emotions. Here is my father during the last decade of his life, away from home.

How we missed him when he went abroad! But then again, I am reminded of all the times he took me and my sisters along with him on tour. It was such fun traveling with him: wonderful concerts, lots of new people to meet, cities to explore and always my father's boundless energy and joy in both his work and time spent with family and friends.

When Leonard Bernstein traveled to Europe, it was as if his batteries were charging. The concerts were, most often, triumphant, and he delighted in making new friends, seeing old friends again and discovering the world through different languages.

This book of photographs is unique in that it shows Leonard Bernstein in the specific contexts of place and age. But, in the end, I am comforted to realize that here is the man I knew and loved—as familiar as if we were playing a word game by the swimming pool. He was a man, after all, who was at home anywhere in the world.

Alexander Bernstein

Alexander Bernstein in his father's apartment
in the Dakota House, New York, 1996

Bernstein's apartment in the Dakota House in New York remained nearly untouched for many years, until it was finally sold in the spring of 1997. I was given the opportunity to photograph it in the fall of 1996, shortly before it was vacated. The contents of the apartment were auctioned at Sotheby's in New York on December 10–11, 1997, and the proceeds donated to the Bernstein Education Through the Arts (BETA) Fund, established by Leonard Bernstein in 1990 in the last year of his life.

Bernstein and John F. Kennedy were Harvard graduates and good friends. Upon hearing that Kennedy had been assassinated, he dedicated his freshly completed symphony, *Kaddish*, to him: "To the Beloved Memory of John F. Kennedy." The second photo on the grand piano shows Bernstein together with his son Alexander.

Leonard Bernstein's apartment in the Dakota House in New York, 1996

Munich Riem Airport, 1987

Contents

"Oh well, some other time." L.B.

There are two kinds of people left in the world; the ones who knew him and the ones who didn't.
The ones who didn't know him include, of course, the ones who may have only *seen* him. When asked, "What was he like?", they invariably stop, gaze, usually smile wistfully (maybe even smirk) and begin a litany of adjectives, mostly surrounded by the phrase, "He was one of the most... I have ever..." And proudly conclude their testament.

The other ones, the ones who did actually know him, when asked the same question, also pause and gaze, but not so much in recollection as in intense focus and scrutiny of the person asking the question, as if in order to determine whether, in fact, that person is qualified to ask or, more importantly, prepared for the answer.
You see, "Lenny"—Leonard Bernstein—overwhelmed! He always did ... he always will.
So what is this great mystery about a person's life, about Lenny's life, that seems to be continually asked? Is it the "what" of his days or the "how" of his talents or the "why" of his strivings? Statistics and presumptions don't give us insight into someone, and certainly not into Lenny. The story does. Not the story about Lenny, but the story Lenny told us over and over again—the story told in every gesture, glance, posture, and musical fantasy in which he took flight. A great artist always tells the great story: the story that is always unique and yet somehow curiously the same through-out generations: The Story of Being.
Lenny had the patience of the saints, but he couldn't stand pretense. You know, the kind of pretending to "be" some-thing, and that something not really "being" after all—which is somehow worse than not having "been" at all.
The creative breath he drew and that we inhaled from him reeked of stronger stuff than one man's ego. It had the musk of time in it, the kind found in old and sage books. It intoxicated one with the simple and profound attempt to tell that moment, any moment, in its context with those emotions and thoughts just as it was and is.
I remember once asking Lenny in my exuberant, youthful, naive way why he thought Mahler started *The Songs of a Wayfarer* right off with such a curious collection of indications: "a triplet over a 2/4 bar in a 4 bar phrase, no-ted as 63 = the ¼ note, and a then fermata! on the bar line! going to the same 2/4 (no rhythm changes) in a 60 = the ¼ motion as the singing begins. The whole question repeats itself in the next phrase as well. I mean really—wow—what notation, what command of rhythm, what subtle articulation ... blah, blah, blah ..." (you can just hear me).
Well, Lenny looked up from his comfortable scotch on a fall Sunday afternoon in Connecticut, a million miles from

Mahler's life and said not unscathingly: "Well, shit, man! Haven't you ever been to a Jewish wedding? You know *Daidle, Deedle, Dum, Yump, Dum ...*" (humming abrasively Mahler's tune), "and then the guy sings ... And he is not happy! Come on! Forget all this crap and just sing!"
And sing *he* did as *I'd* never sung before. You see when you made music with Lenny, or especially sang with Lenny, it was one voice.
The storytelling, truth-seeking something that is written in every memory or image of Lenny brought us a kind of transcendence often used to describe his music making. But it was really born of a passionate need for others to travel with him past the one moment to the many of moments to which we all belong, and past the ego of one to the ego center of the "All," to embrace together the essence of compassion or co-passion and love: the Community of Being.
Quoting the oft-used phrase, "a picture be worth a thou-sand words," what you have in your hands is a small encyclopedia of a small part of a large life of a small man with a huge soul, who, in some small way, wished a larger consciousness and passion for us small people on this small planet in this large universe ... "Oh well, some other time." L.B.

Thomas Hampson

Heights of Rapture—Depths of Melancholy

It is an honor and a challenge for me to write some introductory words for this wonderful volume on Leonard Bernstein. As many of his friends and contemporaries knew him much longer and perhaps better than I did, I would like to limit myself to my most powerful reminiscences of the years we played together—the last decade of Bernstein's life, during which Thomas R. Seiler also captured his photographic images of their travels together.

I was first personally introduced to Bernstein at a dinner in 1980 after one of his concerts in Munich. The evening was aglow and when he told me that he was planning to do *Tristan* with me, I was so delighted I could hardly speak. The work began between Christmas and New Year's. It was an enormous project with three acts spread over January, April and November. That I would give birth to my daughter Sara that same year, just six weeks before the third act, was unbeknown even to me as we started *Tristan*.

The live concerts in the Herkulessaal with Bernstein's much beloved Bavarian Radio Symphony Orchestra were broadcasted simultaneously in radio and television, as well as being recorded for video and LP. We singers stood on a high platform behind the orchestra. Each of us had a whole bouquet of microphones in front of us and were expected to gesticulate a little as well. An expectant atmosphere weighed on the entire event and on each individual, but it soon became clear that the higher the voltage, the better the maestro felt.

Bernstein once said: "When I conduct Beethoven, I don't care whether I conduct the way Beethoven would have conducted. What's important is that I'm convinced that what I've done is in the spirit of Beethoven, even if I know that Beethoven would have done it differently. One is not a slave to a work of the past, but a creator, here and now!" In the same breathtaking way, Bernstein took possession of *Tristan*. As it was Peter Hofmann's debut in this role, the maestro was touchingly attentive in his efforts to help him past all the precipices and chasms of the part. Yet in so doing he was forced to restrain his own urge to identify with the Tristan role. He seemed to try to compensate for this by drawing all the more on the depths of Isolde's character. He sang and hummed my cantilenas along with me, his mind focused inwards. As we came to Isolde's central phrase, "*Er sah mir in die Augen*," he brought the orchestra almost—as it seemed to me—to a halt through an excessive rallentando. I went on the offensive and protested: "Lenny, you're not leaving me anything for my ritardando! I'm Isolde, you don't have to be everyone!" He was a "zealous god," and after this first act, a slightly quarrelsome atmosphere smoldered between us.

After one rehearsal, Lenny sat down at a harpsichord that happened to be there. Dressed in a white bathrobe with a cigarette holder in his mouth, he made a fascinating foray into the harmonic structure of the *Tristan* score. Unforgettable! In Vienna, Munich and Bregenz I performed his third symphony, *Kaddish*, together with Bernstein himself, who corrected my Hebrew unrelentingly. He had premiered this moving piece with his deceased wife, Felicia Montealegre. Lenny accompanied me on the piano at several charity galas in New York in which we performed his own vocal works or Marlene Dietrich's evergreens from *Der Blaue Engel*. Lenny would be dressed in a sassy white tuxedo with glistening Lurex trousers and patent leather buckled shoes and I would be in Marlene-look with a midnight-blue evening

dress, hat, cigarette holder and rhinestone-studded high heels. We had a load of fun; indeed, parties were held whenever the occasion called for it, for example after one wonderful performance of *West Side Story* on Broadway to which Peter Hofmann and I were invited by Lenny.
As I leaf through this volume and look at these so very characteristic photographs, I think of the stories from Bernstein's life that he liked to tell late at night. The intoxicating effect of life and profound melancholy sapped the substance of his volcanic temperament. Ruthless exploitation of his character deeply scored the bedrock. I can remember how he told us in New York that a team of doctors was attempting to teach him how to sleep again.
Like almost no one else, Bernstein bequeathed to young people the Olympian fire, the flame of musical passion. His open-mindedness ("There is no such thing as U- and E-Musik, only good and bad music!"), his own compositions, his great admiration for the Beatles—all these confirmed his "credibility" and youthfulness of heart to the younger generation. In 1997, when I performed a lieder recital with Christoph Eschenbach in Japan at the Pacific Festival—which Bernstein had initiated in 1990 for young musicians from throughout the world (and at which he allegedly once more felt happy and alive shortly before his death)—we played one of his works for voice, piano and cello (*Dream with me*) as part of the encore. The first cellist from the Vienna Philarmonic (Friedrich Dolezal) had come over from another auditorium to do this encore with us after his own concert had finished. When I announced the piece, a cheer went up in the young audience. The spark of the Bernstein name had spontaneously combusted.

Hildegard Behrens

Rehearsals for *Tristan und Isolde*, Herkulessaal, Munich, 1981

<
Choir rehearsal room at Bavarian Radio, Munich, 1981

With the repetiteur Günther von Noé

Hildegard Behrens and Peter Hofmann

During a concert tour in 1981 to perform his *Kaddish*, Lenny and I
flew together from Munich to Zurich. While Lenny, in his elegant cape
with his white silk scarf and silver cigarette holder, took his seat in
the front row of first class, I made my way through the curtain into the
economy section. Everyone seated already, the curtain suddenly
opened and Lenny, peeking through, called out in his smoky voice:
"What's the matter, darling, can't you afford to fly first class?"
Swallowing my pride, I answered with a laugh: "Sure I can, Lenny, but
you can't afford to fly economy!" The curtain closed quickly and
we took off.

Hildegard Behrens

Rehearsals for *Tristan und Isolde*, choir
rehearsal room at Bavarian Radio, Munich, 1981

Rehearsals for *Tristan und Isolde*, Herkulessaal, Munich, 1981

The pinnacle of Bernstein's long-standing collaboration with Bavarian Radio was the legendary 1981 production of *Tristan* for television and record in which Hildegard Behrens played Isolde and Peter Hofmann Tristan. We were fascinated by Lenny's great seriousness, his positively philosophical understanding of Wagner's music and his uncompromising interpretation of this love drama. At the end of the production as we listened in the studio, we felt speechless and moved—Lenny was sitting in front of the score, weeping. "*Unbewußt, höchste Lust.*"

Martin Wöhr

With Martin Wöhr in the recording studio
of the Herkulessaal, Munich, 1981

With Charlie Harmon, Musikverein, Vienna, 1982

September 1982, the Musikverein, Vienna. A rehearsal with the Vienna Philharmonic has just ended. The performances and recordings that month included Brahms' Violin Concerto (with Gidon Kremer), Double Concerto (with Kremer and Mischa Maisky), Second Symphony, and Second Serenade; Mozart's Overture to *Don Giovanni*; and the Adagio from Mahler's Tenth Symphony.

These were the last conducting and recording sessions before Leonard Bernstein would try to metamorphose himself into the composer of the opera *A Quiet Place*. Many times he said that the major difficulty in effecting the change from conductor to composer was in emptying his head of the music of "all those other composers," in this case Brahms, Mozart, Mahler. Beneath the fatigue on this face is an introspection that could be mistaken for the blankness of complete exhaustion. But this is the mask of someone listening to an interior music. The rehearsal has finished, but the sound continues inside Mr. Bernstein's head.

The towel I've just placed on his shoulders looks like a mantle, terry cloth masquerading as royal ermine; more aptly, it's the post-bout gear of a prize fighter. Its whiteness heightens the otherworldly obscurity inside the Musikverein late on a fall afternoon. It's the dimness of an old library, fostering quiet rational thoughts. This is the same light Brahms would have seen at the rehearsals of his Second Symphony in this building 105 years earlier. The music of thought pervades here, and the very air of the Musikverein weighs on one's shoulders like a mantle.

The shoulder of the concertmaster Prof. Gerhart Hetzel is in the left corner; he's politely asking Leonard Bernstein a fairly intense musical question. I have no doubt that Mr. Bernstein is playing the questioned passage in his head. I'm listening in, with an affected hand under my chin, unconsciously trying to make myself look as serious as possible as I try to comprehend not only the question but also Prof. Hetzel's elegantly polite German. What I remember is that in the works by Brahms, there was articulation in the strings that Mr. Bernstein had asked for from the podium ... this was part of my job, to put these conductorial markings into the orchestra parts.

In a few weeks, Mr. Bernstein would be at his home in Fairfield, Connecticut, where over the winter he would write *A Quiet Place*. Yet the music of this rehearsal and of those concerts (there was a short tour with the Vienna Philharmonic to Munich and Berlin) and in fact of every concert that year would remain clearly in his mind with complete recall of every detail.

I look at this photograph now and think: Brahms, Bernstein, and faithful Prof. Hetzel are gone, and where is the music they made? It still sounds in my ear, where I also can hear Prof. Hetzel's question and Mr. Bernstein's answer. While the essence of music may lie in its transient existence, the lesson of a photograph is that our memories may be what bind us to one another.

Yet memory is as transient as music.

Charlie Harmon

With August Everding,
Prinzregententheater,
Munich, 1983

... You never settled for the status quo. Your passion is the imagination. Imagination is the path to your suffering, but also awakens your hope, that hope, that principle of hope that has always moved you—and us. For you, music is always an unanswered question. And your answer is always Yes. The courage required for this positivism, which is more than cheap faith in the future, to say Yes today when people believe that No is the only word that can be uttered, this Yes that you transform into a No when it threatens the Yes: this Yes is the answer to a question and is not a statement. It is not a tranquilizer, nor is it a harmonizing bridge spanning an abyss. Your second symphony describes the age of anxiety. Your hope bides its time on the lee side of your despair. You hope that in *your* ninth, the age of anxiety will be transformed into the age of peace. Your Yes is so courageous because it bears up under the scorn of those who have made a profession of saying No. What's important to you is the *platform*, even if some ridicule it as being more like a *platitude.* In the search for truth, that bacchanalian carousal, as Hegel put it, in which no one is sober, in this search, one needs to be "drunk from the expanse of the mind." You have enough courage to keep telling your pupils and listeners that imagination is not enough if ability is lacking. You are a geyser—too hot for some, too uncontainable for others, yet you are also often a "Quiet Place."
But you have confessed: "I'm always marching for something." And this being on the move has kept you young and attracted young people ...

August Everding

Excerpt from a eulogy delivered on the occasion of the award of the Ernst von Siemens Musikpreis to Leonard Bernstein in 1987

With August Everding in the Prinzregententheater before its reopening,
Munich, 1983.

Bernstein conducted his first concert in Munich at the Prinzregententheater
in 1948. Built in 1900/1901, the theater was closed in 1964 due to
its poor condition. It was August Everding, General Director of the Bavarian
State Theaters since 1982, who finally succeeded in putting through
the long-delayed plans for renovation and reopening.

The theater was reopened in a form referred to as the "small solution" in
1988. Construction for the "grand solution" was completed in 1996.

<
Vienna, 1984

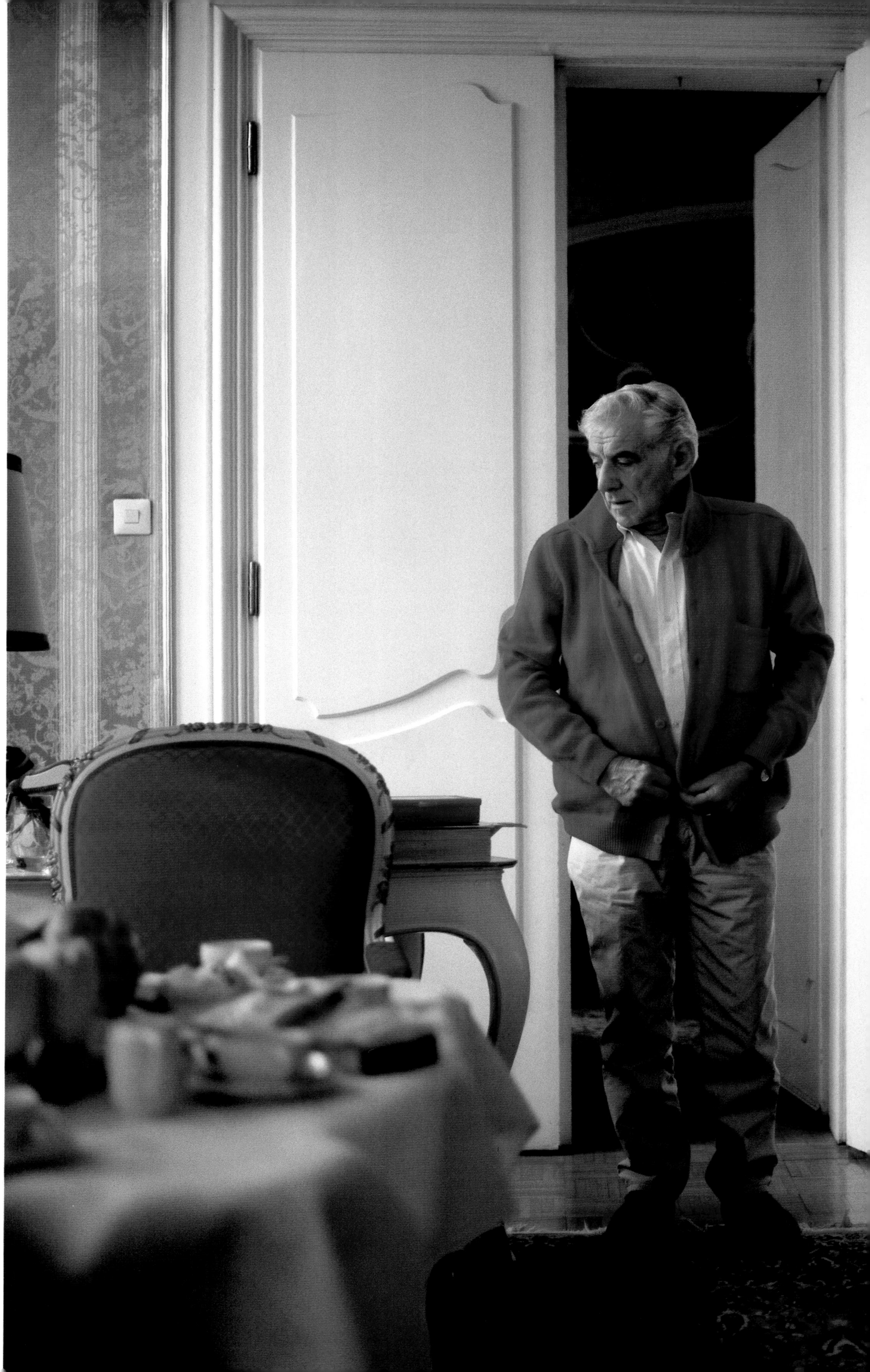

Hotel Sacher, Vienna, 1983

With Domiziana Giordano, Loden Plankl, Vienna, 1983

In Vienna we went and found a traditional Austrian jacket. I cannot remember whether Lenny bought it or not, as it was mere excuse not to think about music and just go out for a walk and relax. Indeed, he loved to be well dressed and had very refined taste. It was on such an occasion that I took one of the very few pictures I have of him. I keep it with me wherever I go, and I think that by now my heart must have the very form of his face.

Domiziana Giordano

Loden Plankl, Vienna, 1983

With Thomas R. Seiler and Franco Amurri following
the visit to Loden Plankl. Photo taken by
Domiziana Giordano with Thomas R. Seiler's camera.

Dressing room at the Musikverein, Vienna, 1983

With Dietlinde Turban,
Gerhart Hetzel and Lorin Maazel
in the dressing room at the
Musikverein following a concert,
Vienna, 1984

Dear Lenny-Maestro,
I completely forgot to tell you that I have planted three cypress trees in my garden
for my three artistic mentors: Böhm—Karajan—Bernstein.
But yours is the biggest!
I am eternally grateful for everything you have taught me beyond music.

Yours, Christa

With Gerhart Hetzel and Christa Ludwig

We always talked about what was special, un-
mistakable, about what was not mainstream
in music—and in so doing there emerged certain
moments with L.B. which occurred spontaneously,
quasi unconsciously, undirected, revealing a
glimpse of the indispensability of music. Mahler's
Fourth in Vienna was one of these moments
(the photo shows our conversations—so often we
came to speak of the Bible, of enigmatic situa-
tions, of small miracles such as this):
Sunday matinee, Musikverein—The milky midday
light shining through the upper row of windows
suddenly flashes up in the same moment that the
(Tölzer) boy soprano stands up in the organ
loft (not previously visible) to begin the fourth
movement. A laser-like swathe of sunlight enriched
with the gold of the organ enshrouds him and
then dissolves on exactly the third-last bar with
the low E-octave by the harp. "*Kein Musik ist
ja nicht auf Erden, die unsrer verglichen kann
werden.*"
Directed? by whom? how? from where?:
L.B. and his world.

Christoph Eschenbach

With Christoph Eschenbach, Hotel Sacher, Vienna, 1984

One sees soon enough in life that virtually all human beings are replaceable, with the single exception of a genius. There have only been a limited number of people in the world of science and politics who, by force of great talent, discoveries and contributions to life itself really seemed to be irreplaceable. The witty and sharp remark in an obituary by Alfred Polgar that somebody "left a gap that replaces him completely" is the other side of the same coin. Oddly enough, it seems that only the evil some humans created in their lifetime was repeated in the same way or worse throughout history. Immune from this are the artists of past and modern times, maybe some towering inventors and scientists. But among the artists of the twentieth century, one stands virtually alone, a total human being who turned even imperfections into appealing assets and made lasting contributions to all our lives. That was the sublime modern musician, Bernstein. His many contributions of genius as a composer, conductor, writer and teacher made

him the first giant artistic figure to survive himself, to continue in full force and vitality beyond his death, with literally hundreds of perfect recordings, ideal interpretations of his own work and the legacy of intelligence and human compassion. Apart from all the work he produced, he created a residue of life unparalleled even among other human beings of genius. He never stopped living.

Robert Lantz

Musikverein, Vienna, 1984

Bernstein "The Magic"

Working with Leonard Bernstein was always an experience.
During rehearsals, he required the musicians to give
everything they had. He also gave everything he had. Lack
of concentration or weak performances were concepts
that simply did not exist, and everyone knew it. The "secret"
behind the absolute dedication of the musicians in
rehearsals and concerts was that Bernstein did not view
the orchestra as a subservient gathering. Instead, he
considered every individual to be a colleague with whom he
wanted to make beautiful music. He didn't act like an
animal trainer or a grand maestro, but saw himself as a
"primus inter pares," for which he was rewarded with
unconditional love.
I can remember one rehearsal—on a Saturday at 5 p.m.—for
which Bernstein was one hour late. After pressing on
with great intensity, he still hadn't got through the work by
the time the official end of the rehearsal had arrived.
He then proposed that the orchestra take a short break
and continue with an open-ended rehearsal until everything
had been worked through. Everybody agreed! No one
would have even begun to think about the hour that had
been lost!
However, during this rehearsal Bernstein did get a little
annoyed when at one point a tempo change wouldn't work
no matter what he tried. He simply couldn't understand why
nobody was responding to him. Then he had an idea.
He said to the orchestra: "Now listen. This change in tempo
is not an issue of my conducting. The tempo comes of its
own accord, if only you would listen to each other! Now
we're going to do it *without* me." He stopped conducting and
left us musicians to rely on our ears ... and it worked!
A magician!

Friedemann Winklhofer

In the dressing room at the Herkulessaal, Munich, 1984

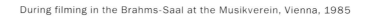
During filming in the Brahms-Saal at the Musikverein, Vienna, 1985

On October 31, 1985, Rudolf Serkin was distinguished with the
"Ehrenringverleihung" of the Vienna Philharmonic.
On that day we were in the Brahms-Saal of the Musikverein,
filming a Unitel production. When the time came, Bernstein went
down to the award ceremony to congratulate his old friend.

With Rudolf Serkin, Musikverein, Vienna, 1985

Rehearsals with the
Vienna Philharmonic,
Musikverein,
Vienna, 1985

My dear, close friend and brilliant, fun-filled
collaborator—Leonard: seeing these fine pictures
reminds me of sitting back with the basses,
watching him at a rehearsal, and hearing him
transform what I thought at first hearing
was perfect into something transcendent when
he was finished.

Betty Comden

With the Vienna Philharmonic, Musikverein, Vienna, 1985

A month after Leonard Bernstein died, there was a memorial concert in Carnegie Hall. In addition to many of the world's most celebrated vocal artists, spokespeople and conductors, the New York Philharmonic was expanded by about fifty people, many of whom came from all over the world at their own expense. In addition, the Westminster Choir with about two hundred people was on stage.
I was invited to participate, which was as great an honor as any that could be bestowed upon me. I sang "To What You Said" from Bernstein's *Songfest*. When I was finished with my excerpt, I went out front and sat in one of the boxes in Carnegie Hall. At one point, apparently a decision was made, and the audience experienced the following: the concert-master gave the downbeat, and the orchestra played the overture to *Candide*. What we saw was the conductor's music stand lighted—but without the conductor. There was not a dry eye in the house!

Chester Ludgin

Rehearsals for excerpts from Richard Wagner's *Ring des Nibelungen*, Vienna State Opera, 1985

At the time of the concert performances of the final scenes from Richard Wagner's operatic cycle *Ring des Nibelungen* at the Vienna State Opera, Bernstein made a film recording of a statement on Wagner at the Sigmund Freud Museum on Berggasse 19, under the direction of Unitel producer Horant Hohlfeld. In his studies of texts and sources related to Wagner, Bernstein had repeatedly come across the latter's apparent depth-psychological problems with his father image: shortly after Richard's birth and the death of her first husband, Wagner's mother had married the highly intelligent Jewish actor Richard Geyer. In a carefully formulated self-analysis, Bernstein also explored the question of how he as a Jew could feel such deep admiration for the music of the composer infamous for his alleged anti-Semitism.

"Please help me, Mr. Freud"; yet Bernstein found no satisfactory answer to his question. The recording ended with a "to be continued" and remained a fragment, one that unfortunately has never been published.

In front of the Sigmund Freud Museum, Vienna, 1985

With Marcel Prawy on the way to the Sigmund Freud Museum, Vienna, 1985

I never called him "Lenny"

When at the peak of our intense collaboration he said to me, "I appreciate your not calling me 'Lenny,'" I knew that my boundless admiration for the genius of my "Maestro" was reciprocated by a trace of friendship. He hated faked buddydom. I had been his fan since his early New York triumphs of 1943. When I produced his musical *Wonderful Town* in 1956 at the Volksoper in Vienna, it was the first production of any theatrical work by Bernstein on the European continent. A profound human relationship followed. From then on, all of Bernstein's stage works—including *West Side Story*, whose German version is my translation— had their continental European premieres as my productions in Vienna.
Bernstein's spirit embraced the entire world of music. His most interesting explanations of Beethoven were given at 3 a.m. in a jazz club, those of jazz in the dressing room of the Großer Musikvereinssaal. Through his TV shows, millions learned the difference between major and minor. He was one of the most important conductors in history. His books contain deepest philosophical thoughts. He was

one of the world's most popular men, yet remained a great unknown—few are familiar with his symphonic works or his chamber music. In *West Side Story*, he raised the art form of the musical to heights it never reached again.
One never left his company without a sentence one remembered forever. Once he told me: "The entire world is *West Side Story*. Everybody hates everybody but two are in love!" Whatever he touched turned to gold. He was Midas, king of music.

Marcel Prawy

P.S. True Bernstein fanatics like me consider *Mass* his most significant work. It was written in 1971 for the opening of the Kennedy Center in Washington, and later I often produced it in Europe. In the summer of 1972, the world-famous impresario Sol Hurok produced *Mass* at the Met. Advance ticket sales were miserable. As I sat next to my depressed friend Hurok during the rehearsals, he whispered in my ear: "Prawy! I think the writing of masses should be left to the Goyim..." After the premiere, *Mass* was a blockbuster at the Met.

In front of the Sigmund Freud Museum, Vienna, 1985

Here Tommy Seiler has captured my image—receiving instructions and waiting for answers—two things I did a lot of in my years traveling with Lenny.

Lenny was always thoughtful, most times considerate (he never called me before 8 a.m. or after midnight), usually digressive in related and very interesting ways, sometimes wanting the questions (and me) to go away. When he was short-tempered, he invariably apologized (often without reason) before he slept. He provided the most interesting hours of my life.

Tommy Seiler was often there—a fly on the wall—recording those many moments of serious fun, taking pictures in an unobtrusive way and being sure that he didn't become part of the picture. This book is such a collection of the joys of my life—and Lenny's!

Harry Kraut

With Harry Kraut in the Sigmund Freud Museum, Vienna, 1985

With Horant Hohlfeld in the Sigmund Freud Museum, Vienna, 1985

It was impossible not to be overwhelmed by Leonard Bernstein's charitable and compassionate nature, and I believe he was the only true great of his time who had no enemies, just thankful friends and admirers. Bernstein loved people and this love was requited a million times over.
I found the following experience unforgettable because it was so typical. For one of his last concerts in Germany, I had to stand in for the camera director at short notice.
I hurriedly made my way to distant Waldsassen, where I met Lenny. He was slightly irritable and greeted me with the words: "I've heard you're going to be my director as of tomorrow," to which I answered, "Yes, Lenny, if you don't have any objections." He replied, "Do I have a choice?"
My jaw almost dropped to my knees. This was not how I had imagined myself being received after having saved the day. Feeling somewhat annoyed, I got on with my work so that the recording of Mozart's *Mass in C-minor* (among other works) could begin the next day. Sitting in the studio van, I started the recording equipment, and radioed the production manager: "Enter maestro, please." Nothing happened. Inquiring as to the whereabouts of the maestro, I was told that he was writing a letter. But before I was able to make any inappropriate remarks that perhaps this was not the right time to be attending to one's correspondence, Bernstein appeared and the concert began.

Suddenly there was a knock on the door of the broadcast van and a little note was handed to me. It said: "Dear Horant, Good luck! I love you. Lenny B." After the concert I went to Lenny to tell him how everything had gone and thank him for the note. I will never forget his answer: "I had the feeling I had hurt you yesterday, which was never my intention. I had only heard about the change of director five minutes before and was irritated at the bad organization and lack of information. Today I had the feeling that before we recorded such a great work, everything had to be okay between us. That's why I wrote you the letter."
Unbelievable, that even before such a difficult concert it was important to this great man to smooth out possible interpersonal tensions and restore harmony.

Horant Hohlfeld

In the Hotel Sacher, Vienna, 1984

A typical "Lenny scene" that shows how much he valued personal contact with the musicians and how excited he was by the enthusiasm of individuals: Vienna, Musikverein, Großer Saal (Main Concert Hall), recording for television. Caught up in Bernstein's enthusiasm and passion, first cellist Friedrich Dolezal began to play so furiously that the nut of his bow caught on the top of his instrument, tearing out a piece of wood as he played. To show Lenny that he could no longer continue, he held up the piece of wood. Lenny snatched it away and tucked it into his breast-pocket. Although it was irreplaceable for the repair of the instrument, Lenny then wanted to keep the precious piece of wood at all costs as a souvenir. Only after long explanations and pleas did he reluctantly return it.

This scene—very refreshing to all of us at the time—is one of my memories of this peerless and, for me, unforgettable conductor of the century.

Alfred Altenburger

Golden Concert Hall at the Musikverein, Vienna, 1984

On Stillness

Stillness is our most intense mode of action. It is in our moments of
deep quiet that is born every idea, emotion, and drive which we eventually
honor with the name of action. Our most emotionally active life is
lived in our dreams, and our cells renew themselves most industriously
in sleep. We reach highest in meditation, and farthest in prayer.
In stillness every human being is great; he is free from the experience of
hostility; he is a poet, and most like an angel.

Leonard Bernstein, 1976

Vienna, 1985

With Krystian Zimerman, Hotel Bristol, Vienna, 1986

Hotel Bristol, Vienna, 1986

With Krystian Zimerman, Hotel Bristol, Vienna, 1986

Eight performances of *Age of Anxiety* in New York. I arrive one evening and Bernstein is sitting there, completely drained and beside himself. He says: "My friend, the tragedy, and he died, can you imagine." I think, My God, has somebody been run over by a bus or what the hell is going on? Then I ask who it was. "A very good friend, a wonderful man and one of the greatest of this century." I reply: "I'm sorry. Do I know him?" Then he says: "Yes, it was J.F.K.."
I was confused, but Bernstein had meant what he said. This particular evening was the twentieth anniversary of John F. Kennedy's death and I sensed that for him it was just like yesterday. He had purposefully worked himself up to this point and—by then I had already known him a long time, my first concert with him was in 1976—I already suspected what was in store for us. So we went out onto the stage and *Age of Anxiety* began. With slow movements and a tragic expression on his face, he turned to the orchestra and began, *te·ee dum, dah dah.* I suddenly realized with dismay—the symphony had begun at half-tempo ...

Krystian Zimerman

With daughter Jamie, Hotel Bristol, Vienna, 1986

Rehearsals for Bernstein's opera
A Quiet Place, Vienna State Opera, 1986

In 1986, Lenny and I presided over a new production of *A Quiet Place* at the Vienna State Opera, he as conductor, I as director.

Many were the travails. After the bombing of Libya by the U.S., we were informed by Austrian security police of a threatened terrorist action against a U.S. installation in Vienna on the day of our opening. A company meeting was called during which the Austrians told us how to seem less American. On opening night, midway through Act III, there was a deafening bang high above the stage. The four principals onstage moved seamlessly ahead, but the pit chorus, all Americans, levitated as one from their folding chairs. It turned out a couple of lighting instruments had exploded high above the stage.

Lenny was very taxed by the complexities of his own score and by the difficulties the ORF orchestra were having with it, and he nearly fainted several times upon reentering the pit. I worked so hard that during rehearsals I completely lost my voice and literally could not phonate, resulting in several midnight trips to a dank clinic where gruesome procedures were performed on my throat by nervous student doctors.

But there were comforts: the take-out dinners from the Sacher brought to me on rolling tables up in the dusty *Probebühne*, the paged curtain spitting forth our American company onto the forestage of that divine theater. The thousands upon thousands of hours spent with Lenny—at pianos and desks and concerts, across rooms and tables and countries, in planes, in pools, in fits of laughter and exhaustion, in now sorely missed friendship.

At the end of the run, during which performances and recording sessions were too tightly scheduled, we were all herded into a big room and fed wieners and beer while Marcel Prawy stood on a table and entertained the troops. We were really really tired and really really proud and really really ready to go home.

Stephen Wadsworth

Stephen Wadsworth at the party following
the last performance of *A Quiet Place*, Vienna, 1986

Rehearsals for Bernstein's opera *A Quiet Place*, Vienna State Opera, 1986

Munich, June 1986
"At four o'clock in the morning." The party around the pool on top of the Hotel Vier Jahreszeiten was over. All friends were strolling home. "You stay!" An order from Leonard Bernstein. "We have to sing our *Embraceable You* before you leave me!"

Lenny called: "How about a quick goodbye sip?" And there we were in his suite in Munich's Hotel Vier Jahreszeiten sitting at a table in front of plates with breakfast-leftovers and half-empty glasses. We had given him a little book as a going-away present. *New York 1932. Sketches by George Grosz*. We: Friedrich Meyer, composer, and my "constant companion" both on the piano and in life. "Margot can finally be called 'Frau Meyer'!" the press wrote on July 21, 1959.
"How many jazzy piano pieces have you written up to now, Frederic?" Lenny asked. "I've a brilliant title for you, *Play Meyer—Forget Czerny*. Subtitle: *Exercises for Adult Beginners!* You could be the German Cole Porter with your kind of music, Meyer!"
"When were you in New York?" he asked me. "In November 1959. It was our honeymoon. Can you remember what you said at our farewell? You had allowed Friedrich to attend all the orchestra rehearsals in Carnegie Hall. In your box no. 62. He sat there every day. When I came to your office to thank you and to say goodbye on December 24, you said, "The next time you come to New York, tell Frederic to bring his toothbrush and his pyjama along to Carnegie Hall and I'll have his bed set up in box 62!"

Margot Hielscher

Munich, May 9, 1948
Leonard Bernstein conducted the Bavarian State Orchestra. After the concert, the American film-officer Colonel Rogers held a reception for the maestro in the "villa" on the grounds of Bavaria Studios.
Lenny sat down at the grand piano and played. Maurice Ravel, then George Gershwin's *Embraceable You*—I knew it and sang along. The maestro looked at me and said: "I never thought that a pretty 'Nazi-girl' would know this song!" It had become late. Bernstein stayed the night in the villa. My residence at that time was in Rottach am Tegernsee, but the host wouldn't let me drive home and offered to let me spend the night in a little guestroom in the attic. As I sneaked up the creaking stairs, the maestro opened his door: "Please, wait a moment. There's something I want to know about you!"
So I told him about my tour with an American army jazz-band through West Germany and Austria in 1945/46. And about how I had been able to buy American records in Berlin as early as 1935. My favorite had been *Girl Crazy*, the George Gershwin musical with the song *Embraceable You*.
And so our wonderful friendship began with this "musical embrace."

Margot Hielscher

With Margot Hielscher and her husband Friedrich Meyer,
Hotel Vier Jahreszeiten, Munich, 1986

With Margot Hielscher after a swimmingpool party,

Hotel Vier Jahreszeiten, Munich, 1986

With Harry Kraut in the dressing room at the Musikverein, Vienna, 1986

With the Countess of Reventlow, Wulfshagen estate,
Schleswig Holstein, 1987.
Leonard Bernstein stayed here during the Schleswig Holstein Festivals
from 1987 to 1989.

Schleswig Holstein, 1987

With Craig Urquhart in Wulfshagen, Schleswig Holstein, 1987

On the Road with Lenny

It was March of 1986. I had been working with the legendary Leonard Bernstein for a few months in New York, but it was now time to travel. My first travel assignment was to prepare to leave for Vienna, where Bernstein was to conduct his opera *A Quiet Place* at the State Opera House. I met with my predecessor and we went over what needed to be transported to Vienna. I use this word advisedly because I had no idea we were to travel with what seemed like the complete contents of Bernstein's large Dakota apartment, packed into fifteen or so pieces of luggage. Perhaps I exaggerate, but not entirely!

Very quickly I learned that Mr. Bernstein had a desire to create a sense of home wherever he went. He would take a small library of his ever beloved books, including various foreign language dictionaries, *The Oxford Book of Poetry*, the complete works of William Shakespeare, *Alice in Wonderland*, his gem-covered Torah, the Bible, numerous crossword puzzle books, unread magazines, various novels, books of nonfiction, biographies, a trunk of musical scores and score paper, pencils, erasers and so on. Perhaps most important were the photographs of his family and friends, which were arranged with love in every single hotel suite he used. Bernstein used the very same hotel suite from year to year—in Vienna, Berlin, Rome, Tel Aviv, Jerusalem, London, Paris, Tokyo. Each hotel kept on file the precise arrangement of the room "to make Lenny feel at home." A specific location was assigned to the grand piano, the dining table, couches and chairs, and his desk. Wherever he went, it was important to him, this sense of home, of family.

New Yorkers, even those Midwest transplants like me, tended to feel that Bernstein was part of the fabric of New York. Because of that, we felt special. I soon learned that New Yorkers were not alone. It was on that first trip to Vienna where I learned that the Viennese also felt the great Bernstein belonged to them. In Vienna as well as in Tel Aviv, Rome, London, Tokyo, Berlin, Paris, Munich, Amsterdam and wherever he traveled, everyone felt the same. He was greeted and honored by heads of state, ambassadors, mayors, priests and rabbis—even royalty—many of whom became his genuine and devoted friends, with whom he often held forth in discourse and spent many late evening together. They all thought that he was theirs!

After every concert he would spend time, sometimes hours, wearing a robe atop his conducting trousers, drinking his favorite Scotch whisky from a silver cup (many of which he gave away as gifts), and smoking cigarettes while signing autographs and receiving his friends and fans. The love he brought with him was returned by the love of these dear friends and fans.

But no matter how large this family was, his heart was never far from his immediate family. Shabbat always meant a telephone call to his mother Jennie, wherever he was. How he always longed to be home with his family, sitting around the Dakota library table, or in the country house in Fairfield, Connecticut, having drinks, playing word games, surrounded by loved ones. Traveling with Lenny taught me how much there is to be thankful for: how Lenny shared of himself and that so many shared with him; that there really is a family of humankind; and how he truly made the world a better place in which to live.

Craig Urquhart

With Craig Urquhart in the dressing room at the concert hall in Lübeck, 1987

On Bernstein's
sixty-ninth birthday,
Salzburg, 1987

Paris, 1987

Paris, 1987

I like to think of Leonard as my closest friend—all right, I'll insist on it—he *was* my closest friend and in many ways my dearest.

I first met him in 1937 when I was an unhealthily stout unemployed son of the Depression in my early twenties and Leonard, aged eighteen, was the musical counselor at a boys' camp in Pittsfield, Massachusetts—Camp Onota. Through the kindness of a buddy, Robert Weil, dramatic counselor at that very camp, I got an invitation to spend two weeks appearing in the camp's big summer festival as the Pirate King in *The Pirates of Penzance,* my first and only way-off-off-off-Broadway stage appearance.

Robert had told me by mail that in the person of young Bernstein, I was about to meet a remarkable musician of near-miraculous skills. I got a free ride from New York City from some kindly parents and arrived at Onota around 10:00 p.m. We pulled up in front of the Social Hall where I immediately encountered young Leonard who at first glance seemed to be no more than twelve years old. "So you're the Adolph Green who knows so much about music," he said instantly. I answered, "Well, I—I..." Then he dragged me inside and sat me near the piano. I was truly embarrassed. It seems my friend Robert had proclaimed my musical knowledge to Leonard and in turn had proclaimed Leonard's to me and both Leonard and I thought the other must be a total fraud of some kind. "I don't really know that much

With Adolph Green and François Valéry, Hôtel de Crillon, Paris, 1988

about music," I mumbled. "I just love it but can't read a note." "I'll play you a short piece by Shostakovich, a sort of dance," he said, "and we'll see if you know it." I sat there uncertainly while he played a rhythmic, somewhat discordant short piece that I tried desperately to identify as he played, but with no success. As he finished Leonard said, "Of course you know this piece well." For a split second I wondered whether I should lie and say yes, but quickly recovering my integrity no matter how humiliating, I mumbled, "Gee, no, I've never heard it before." No sooner had I said this than Leonard leaped from the piano and threw his arms around me, kissing me at least a dozen times. "It was an improvisation. You're the first one who's heard me play this year and

didn't say he knew it intimately." We then spent the rest of the night walking about the Onota grounds singing and screaming a musical repertoire from Bach to Bartok. I quickly learned that young Leonard was a most extraordinarily gifted musician, composer and performer of all kinds of music—popular as well as classical—and though I had no authority to proclaim him as such, I knew he would flourish in time as a giant of music.

Adolph Green

Galerie Richelieu, Louvre, Paris, 1989

Paris, July 16, 1989.

In the evening, Bernstein was to conduct *Roméo et Juliette* by Berlioz at one of the opening
concerts of the Bastille opera in honor of the 200th anniversary of the French Revolution.
That day, we visited the Louvre and were privileged to see the Galerie Richelieu—open to the
public only later—where, until recently, the Ministry of Finance had been accommodated.
Toward the end of our visit, shortly before I took the pictures on this and the next two pages,
a messenger agitatedly rushed up the stairs of the Galerie Richelieu to tell Bernstein that
Maestro Herbert von Karajan had died that day in Anif near Salzburg.
Before the beginning of the concert on that same evening, Bernstein informed the audience
of the death of his great colleague. For all, the report came as a complete shock.

Galerie Richelieu, Louvre, Paris, 1989

>
Rue de Rivoli, Paris, 1989

Lenny was not only an inspiration to accomplished and
distinguished musicians, he was also a vital force to the young
would-be composer or instrumentalist. He was crucial to
music in the twentieth century and I am happy to have worked
with him, although, sadly, only for one film.

Stanley Donen

Hôtel de Crillon, Paris, 1989

Hôtel de Crillon, Paris, 1989

Leonard Bernstein erupted into my life one beautiful summer evening in 1946 in the company
of Nadia Boulanger, whom my mother had invited to dinner at her home on Rue Villejust
(now Rue Paul Valéry).

I had no idea that he was coming, and I had no idea who he was. But I was immediately struck
by his presence, by the gift of empathy that emanated from him and the intensity of his gaze, which
betrayed intelligence, a sense of humor and a certain gentleness tinged with melancholy.
Dispensing with the rituals of introduction and without a single glance at the Impressionist pain-
tings on the walls, he dragged me to the Erard baby grand, a rather old one that sounded like
an upright. Having barely touched the keys of the somewhat vaguely tuned instrument, he lowe-
red the cover and was about to stand up when I told him that Debussy, Ravel, Darius Milhaud
and André Gide (playing four-handed with my mother) had also played this same slightly yellowed
piano. "Oh, my God!" he said, and immediately intoned the first movement of Bach's fifth
Brandenburg Concerto, playing it as kind of medley from memory with marvelous musical feeling.
When he had finished, my mother (who, like Nadia, had once studied under Raoul Pugno)
approached him, saying: "That's what I call music." Bernstein suddenly wrapped his arms around
this already aging woman and, with a certain sense of respect, pressed his lips to her cheek
for a moment.

It was strange that, despite the friendship that had developed between us, we ran into each other
rather seldom after this encounter, and usually by coincidence, because of our different
occupations. In London, New York, The Hague, Monaco, Salzburg and Paris—he giving his concerts
and I attending some international conference—we made an effort to get together whenever
possible.

And then one last time... We were alone on the terrace of the Crillon, and he suddenly made a
remark that I would never forget: "I think there is something very special between you and me.
I can't think why..."

I answered: "I think so, too. Perhaps because our paths are so different... In any case, I know that
it will always be so." And it was the last time!

François Valéry

With François Valéry, Hôtel de Crillon, Paris, 1989

Leonard Bernstein: what was he to me? He was a lighthouse. A lighthouse in music, in literature, in philosophy, in languages, in humaneness, in religion, in politics. I did not always share his views but that was of no importance. That he made me understand my own views better was what mattered.
He died nine years ago. For me he is still here. Not as a lighthouse anymore (though he still lights my thoughts when I read his books, his lectures, his letters) but as a star.
As one of those stars whose light reaches our planet long after they have ceased to exist.

Peter Weiser

With Peter Weiser and Michael Tilson Thomas, Hôtel de Crillon, Paris, 1989

Leonard Bernstein was an inspirational mentor and friend for generations of musicians. Uncompromising in his standards, patient and generous with his time and attention, he made a worldwide musical family that always rejoiced to be together again. Whether in Vienna, Paris, Sapporo, San Francisco, or Tel Aviv, there was always a sense of homecoming and gratefulness to be in one another's company again and to be making music with the highest sense of purpose and devotion. We miss him.

Michael Tilson Thomas

With Judith Pisar in front of the Hôtel de Crillon, Paris, 1989

With Harry Kraut and Judith Pisar,
Hôtel de Crillon, Paris, 1989

Lenny's Polonaise

In 1989, Lenny invited my husband to Poland to participate
in the international concert commemorating the fiftieth
anniversary of the outbreak of World War II. We all congrega-
ted in Warsaw a few days before the September 1 event—
Lenny, Lukas Foss, Nela Rubinstein, Harry Kraut, Barbara
Hendricks, Michael Barrett, Humphrey Burton, Hermann Prey,
Liv Ullmann, Samuel Pisar and myself.
After our first dinner in the hotel restaurant—washed down
with considerable quantities of Polish vodka—Lenny glided
toward the huge, white lacquered piano in the middle of the
room. A very agitated maître d'hôtel stopped him in his tracks
with the admonition "the cocktail pianist gets very upset if
anyone touches his piano." Lenny, for once, was speechless.
Whereupon Nela Rubinstein, famous in Poland for being
the widow of Arthur, interceded with vehemence: "Do you
know who this is?" After an animated argument in Polish, the
poor man finally gave in, and we were off for a good hour
of Chopin. Never had this sedate dining room seen or heard
anything like it.
The next night, we all headed back to the restaurant for an
encore ... but this time the maître d'hôtel refused to let us in:
his cocktail pianist had thrown a fit, insisting that the piano
had been put out of tune by a loud group of Americans.

Judith Pisar

It was April 1990 in Munich, following Bernstein's final performance with the Bavarian Radio Symphony Orchestra. Our thoughts, like the weather, were chilled and soggy. None of us knew the truth behind his nagging "flu"; the litany of hypochondriac complaints, that smoker's hack and the asthmatic gasp were uncomfortable yet familiar leitmotifs in daily life with the maestro. And really, we were all suffering varying degrees of colds that week of Mozart masses—the higher the voice, the worse the affliction.

Yet, many had noticed something new and unnerving. In the progression from rehearsal to concert, he was *losing* energy and desire instead of soaring. Suddenly, Leonard Bernstein could walk into a room and not be noticed. The dance on the podium was becoming a riveting struggle; off the podium, the dancer was shuffling. Perhaps we who were there to watch over him hoped that our own willpower would prove as infectious as the elements. We were desperate for him to keep going: life with Leonard Bernstein was simply too much fun. What pupil could fail after he sent you onstage with a clamp on the shoulders and a kick in the rear? What ovation

With the Countess of Reventlow in the dressing room at the Herkulessaal after Bernstein's last concert in Germany, Munich, 1990

would ever match the embrace waiting when you came back off? Who would not gladly pass up a good night's sleep when he asked you to "teach me everything *you* know about the piece, and then I'll teach you everything *I* know about the piece?"—or invited you to discuss the world with him, perhaps mentioning a few days later, "You know, you did say one intelligent thing..." You lived for that!

Life with L.B. was continually that moment in *The Wizard of Oz* when the tornado sets us down in a world of color, magic and pioneering balloons. When our wizard left, we woke up to a landscape of mundane grayness.

Mark Stringer

Leonard Bernstein
leaving the
Herkulessaal together
with Mark Stringer,
Munich, 1990

My acquaintance with Leonard Bernstein began in the
summer of 1985, following a concert of the European
Community Youth Orchestra in the Viennese Staatsoper
in which my son Alvaro Palmen played as a violinist.
As so often before, after the concert Lenny invite some
guests to his room in the Hotel Sacher where—how
could it be otherwise—we made a lot of music. I had the
great pleasure of singing excerpts from Puccini's
La Bohème while Lenny accompanied me. We often met
up with friends this way, avidly discussing different
topics and playing music together after concerts in Bonn,
Vienna, Munich, Berlin or Diessen am Ammersee.
At Easter in 1990, my sons and I went to see a performance of Mozart's *Mass in C-minor* with Bernstein
conducting the Bavarian Radio Symphony Orchestra.
Afterwards we went up to Lenny's suite. These pictures
are an exact reflection of our merry get-together in
the Hotel Vier Jahreszeiten in Munich, where we sang
excerpts from Bizet's *Carmen* and French and German
lieder. Apart from several telephone conversations
until the summer of 1990, this meeting, several months
before his death, was unfortunately our last.

Lia Montoya-Palmen

With Lia Montoya-Palmen, Hotel Vier Jahreszeiten, Munich, 1990

For over thirty-one years Leonard Bernstein was a very special friend—
the older brother I never had, the favorite cousin I always wanted—a very
special friend who also happened to be a genius.
The photos in this book bring back so many memories of this man who
gave honor and purpose to American artists. The Danes have a
wonderful expression: "To live in hearts we leave behind is not to die..."
Leonard Bernstein could never die—he lives in too many hearts.

Schuyler Chapin

Hotel Vier Jahreszeiten, Munich, 1990

Thomas R. Seiler's last photos of Leonard Bernstein

These photographs bring back so many memories of special loving moments
that are part of a private legacy of long friendship. All these photos are Lenny, and,
once again, as if it were needed, they remind us of that which we have no more.

Isaac Stern

Hôtel de Crillon, Paris, 1989

Lenny, Lenny Bernstein.
Some would call him Lenny, others Leonardo ... "what's in a name? A rose by any other name
would smell as sweet ..." (Shakespeare).
But there is the crux, the nut, the nuclear grain of the whole microcosmos that was
Leonard Bernstein, the man, the legend, the artist, the intellect—this unfathomable, endless
store of knowledge, memories—a living encyclopedia of worldly intimate experiences. The capital
energy cumulator and distributor to wherever and whatever needed it.
We all felt somehow like his sons, his daughters, fathers, mothers, brothers and sisters—it was
like a mutual life source that assured and reassured us at all times and occasions.
A source, a continuity. Therefore the image of this "love of life" man, translated, expressed
through music or just human relations—is there—now, even if he—Lenny, Leonardo—
is not there in flesh, blood and bones.
Somehow he is within us.
Thank you for having been and for continuing to be this multiple, kaleidoscopic person, warm,
real, extravagant, and simple.
As only you could have been, Lenny.

Ivry Gitlis

With Ivry Gitlis, Le Bourget Airport, Paris, 1989

A few weeks before Lenny died we were having a very late breakfast. He was in a rather pensive mood and I asked him what he was thinking about. "I'm writing my eulogy," he declared. "Cut down in the prime of his youth." "Great first line," I said. "What comes next?" "Ah ha—That's up to you." So...

Lenny, Felicia and I had a more than forty-year, crazy, vertummelte [sic], mixed up relationship—if that's the right word. Sometimes it was rather sweet... I remember on the opening night of *West Side Story*, Lenny was walking down the aisle and he bent over and whispered to me, "I've stolen a line from the second movement of Beethoven's Fifth Piano Concerto." When the show was over I went backstage and asked, "What about the tune from *Götterdämmerung* at the end?" "Oh," he said, "that I knew you would recognize..."

But anecdotes and funnies aside, what I really want to tell you about are Lenny's last days. From the very beginning of the bad troubles last April, he never wanted to impose his sickness on his family or his friends. How many times did we all hear him ask us to help him help himself to go... "without creative energy there was no going on... This life has no dignity—no form." If you asked him what he wanted... "I want an unmessy exit." What can I get you Lenny? "Give me back my breath."

But with all the pain, and it was great, he never lost that mind or his quicksilver wit. When Michael Tilson Thomas, sitting at his knees, told him, "Lenny, I love you very much," Lenny shot back, "You sure picked a fine time to tell me."

He never lost his passion for Jewish learning. One evening, Shirley read the preface to *The book of J* and the next afternoon, he casually remarked to me, "I guess it's about time we had a go at the other one." "At what?" "The Book of Job that is."—Oy—Well I got through five chapters before he stopped me with: "That's enough of that."

And even after death he never lost his adoring public. The funeral cortège, complete with police escort, was forced to slow down somewhere in Brooklyn at a construction site, and the hard-hats stood there waving, "Bye Lenny—goodbye Lenny."

Lauren Bacall, Michael Wager,
Herolyn Blackwell, Betty Comden,
Adolph Green, Jamie Bernstein,
Nina Bernstein, Alexander Bernstein,
Schuyler Chapin, Isaac Stern
(from left to right) at the charity
gala on the eve of the auction of
Leonard Bernstein's estate,
Sotheby's, New York, 1997

Everybody knows that when Lenny was good he was very, very incredible, and when he was bad he was very, very incredible. On the Saturday night before he died, we actually fought. Helping him to bed, I felt a crumpled pack of cigarettes in his pyjama pocket. "Don't you touch those you shit." "If I'm a shit, what are you Lenny?" "A fool," he said. "What would you rather be?" I asked. "A fool," he repeated. But then he relented and handed me the pack, but warning: "Don't you dare hide them, I don't want to feel like a prisoner in my own home." "I see that compromises your autonomy Lenny." "That's right." "Lenny, what exactly is autonomy?" At that, he exploded, "This is no time for philosophic discussion."
It wasn't. That night it was very bad and at one moment he cried out, "Oh, please God, bless me with oblivion." Sunday morning, he was more reflective. "If I should die this week, what was it all about. My life. Did it mean anything? Did I make people happier?"
That evening, Sean Cahill, his physician's son and I were helping him from his bed to his chair. He leaned heavily on us, then raised himself for an instant and said: "What is this?" and collapsed in our arms. That was it ... he was dead ... It was so sudden ... so shocking ... "What is this?" I suppose you can read anything you can imagine into those words. What is this indeed, it was his end. The end of an era and the end of my dearest friend. I shall miss him all the days of my life.

Michael Wager

Excerpt from a eulogy spoken by Michael Wager at Bernstein's funeral at the Dakota and later at the Majestic theater

PROPERTY FROM THE ESTATE OF
LEONARD BERNSTEIN
AUCTION: DECEMBER 10-11

Leonard Bernstein:
August 25, 1918–October 14, 1990

Leonard Bernstein was born in Lawrence, Massachusetts. He took piano lessons as a boy and attended the Garrison and Boston Latin Schools. At Harvard University, he studied with Walter Piston, Edward Burlingame-Hill, and A. Tillman Merritt, among others. Before graduating in 1939, he made an unofficial conducting debut with his own incidental music to *The Birds*, and directed and performed in Marc Blitstein's *The Cradle Will Rock*. Then at the Curtis Institute of Music in Philadelphia, he studied piano with Isabella Vengerova, conducting with Fritz Reiner, and orchestration with Randall Thompson.

In 1940, he studied at the Boston Symphony Orchestra's newly created summer institute, Tanglewood, with the orchestra's conductor, Serge Koussevitzky. Bernstein later became Koussevitzky's conducting assistant.

Bernstein was appointed to his first permanent conducting post in 1943, as Assistant Conductor of the New York Philharmonic. On November 14, 1943, Bernstein substituted on a few hours notice for the ailing Bruno Walter at a Carnegie Hall concert, which was broadcast nationally on radio, receiving critical acclaim. Soon orchestras worldwide sought him out as a guest conductor. In 1945 he was appointed Music Director of the New York City Symphony Orchestra, a post he held until 1947. After Serge Koussevitzky died in 1951, Bernstein headed the orchestral and conducting departments at Tanglewood, teaching there for many years. In 1951 he married the Chilean actress and pianist, Felicia Montealegre. He was also visiting music professor and head of the Creative Arts Festivals at Brandeis University in the early 1950s.

Bernstein became Music Director of the New York Philharmonic in 1958. From then until 1969 he led more concerts with the orchestra than any previous conductor. He subsequently held the lifetime title of Laureate Conductor, making frequent guest appearances with the orchestra. More than half of Bernstein's 400-plus recordings were made with the New York Philharmonic. Bernstein traveled the world as a conductor. Immediately after World War II, in 1946, he conducted in London and at the International Music Festival in Prague. In 1947 he conducted in Tel Aviv, beginning a relationship with Israel that lasted until his death. In 1953, Bernstein was the first American to conduct opera at the Teatro alla Scala in Milan: Cherubini's *Medea* with Maria Callas. Bernstein was a leading advocate of American composers, particularly Aaron Copland. The two remained close friends for life. As a young pianist, Bernstein performed Copland's *Piano Variations* so often he considered the composition his trademark. Bernstein programmed and recorded nearly all of the Copland orchestral works—many of them twice. He devoted several televised *Young People's Concerts* to Copland, and gave the premiere of Copland's *Connotations*, commissioned for the opening of Philharmonic Hall (now Avery Fisher Hall) at Lincoln Center in 1962.

While Bernstein's conducting repertoire encompassed the standard literature, he may be best remembered for his performances and recordings of Haydn, Beethoven, Brahms, Schumann, Sibelius and Mahler. Particularly notable were his performances of the Mahler symphonies with the New York Philharmonic in the 1960s, sparking a renewed interest in the works of Mahler.

Inspired by his Jewish heritage, Bernstein completed his first large-scale work: Symphony No. 1: *Jeremiah* (1943). The piece was first performed with the Pittsburgh Symphony Orchestra in 1944, conducted by the composer, and received the New York Music Critics' Award. Koussevitzky premiered Bernstein's Symphony No. 2: *The Age of Anxiety* with the Boston Symphony Orchestra, Bernstein as piano soloist. His Symphony No. 3: *Kaddish*, composed in 1963, was premiered by the Israel Philharmonic Orchestra. *Kaddish* is dedicated "To the Beloved Memory of John F. Kennedy."

Other major compositions by Bernstein include *prelude, fugue & riffs* for solo clarinet and jazz ensemble (1949); *Serenade* for violin, strings and percussion (1954); *Symphonic Dances from West Side Story* (1960); *Chichester Psalms* for chorus, boy soprano and orchestra (1965); *Mass: A Theater Piece for Singers, Players and Dancers,* commissioned for the opening of the John F. Kennedy Center for the Performing Arts in Washington, D.C., and first produced there in 1971; *Songfest,* a song cycle for six singers and orchestra (1977); *Divertimento* for orchestra (1980); *Halil* for solo flute and small orchestra (1981); *Touches* for solo piano (1981); *Missa Brevis* for singers and percussion (1988); *Thirteen Anniversaries* for solo piano (1988); *Concerto for Orchestra: Jubilee Games* (1989); and *Arias and Barcarolles* for two singers and piano duet (1988). Bernstein also wrote a one-act opera, *Trouble in Tahiti*, in 1952, and its sequel, the three-act opera, *A Quiet Place* in 1983. He collaborated with choreographer Jerome Robbins on three major ballets: *Fancy Free* (1944) and *Facsimile* (1946) for the American Ballet theater; and *Dybbuk* (1975) for the New York City Ballet. He composed the score for the award-winning movie *On the Waterfront* (1954) and incidental music for two Broadway plays: *Peter Pan* (1950) and *The Lark* (1955). Bernstein contributed substantially to the Broadway musical stage. He collaborated with Betty Comden and Adolph Green on *On The Town* (1944) and *Wonderful Town* (1953). In collaboration with Richard Wilbur and Lillian Hellman and others he wrote *Candide* (1956). Other versions of *Candide* were written in association with Hugh Wheeler, Stephen Sondheim et al. In 1957 he again collaborated with Jerome Robbins, Stephen Sondheim, and Arthur Laurents on the landmark musical *West Side Story*, also made into the Academy Award-winning film. In 1976 Bernstein and Alan Jay Lerner wrote *1600 Pennsylvania Avenue*. Festivals of Bernstein's music have been produced throughout the world. In 1978 the Israel Philharmonic sponsored a festival commemorating his years

of dedication to Israel. The Israel Philharmonic also bestowed on him the lifetime title of Laureate Conductor in 1988. In 1986 the London Symphony Orchestra and the Barbican Centre produced a Bernstein Festival. The London Symphony Orchestra in 1987 named him Honorary President. In 1989 the city of Bonn presented a Beethoven/Bernstein Festival. In 1985 the National Academy of Recording Arts and Sciences honored Leonard Bernstein with the Lifetime Achievement Grammy Award. He won eleven Emmy Awards in his career. His televised concert and lecture series started with the *Omnibus* program in 1954, followed by the extraordinary *Young People's Concerts with the New York Philharmonic* in 1958, which extended over fourteen seasons. Among his many appearances on the PBS series *Great Performances* was the eleven-part acclaimed *Bernstein's Beethoven*. In 1989, Bernstein and others commemorated the 1939 invasion of Poland in a worldwide telecast from Warsaw.

Bernstein's writings were published in *The Joy of Music* (1959), *Leonard Bernstein's Young People's Concerts* (1961), *The Infinite Variety of Music* (1966), and *Findings* (1982). Each has been widely translated. He gave six lectures at Harvard University in 1972–1973 as the Charles Eliot Norton Professor of Poetry. These lectures were subsequently published and televised as *The Unanswered Question*. Bernstein always rejoiced in opportunities to teach young musicians. His master classes at Tanglewood were famous. He was instrumental in founding the Los Angeles Philharmonic Institute in 1982. He helped create a world class training orchestra at the Schleswig Holstein Music Festival. He founded the Pacific Music Festival in Sapporo, Japan. Modeled after Tanglewood, this international festival was the first of its kind in Asia and continues to this day. Bernstein received many honors. He was elected in 1981 to the American Academy of Arts and Letters, which gave him a Gold Medal. The National Fellowship Award in 1985 applauded his life-long support of humanitarian causes. He received the MacDowell Colony's Gold Medal; medals from the

Beethoven Society and the Mahler Gesellschaft; the Handel Medallion, New York City's highest honor for the arts; a Tony Award (1969) for Distinguished Achievement in the Theater; and dozens of honorary degrees and awards from colleges and universities. He was presented ceremonial keys to the cities of Oslo, Vienna, Bersheeva and the village of Bernstein, Austria, among others. National honors came from Italy, Israel, Mexico, Denmark, Germany (the Great Merit Cross), and France (Chevalier, Officer and Commandeur of the Legion d'Honneur). He received the Kennedy Center Honors in 1980.

World peace was a particular concern of Bernstein. Speaking at Johns Hopkins University in 1980 and the Cathedral of St. John the Divine in New York in 1983, he described his vision of global harmony. *His Journey for Peace* tour to Athens and Hiroshima with the European Community Orchestra in 1985 commemorated the 40th anniversary of the atom bomb. In December 1989, Bernstein conducted the historic *Berlin Celebration Concerts* on both sides of the Berlin Wall as it was being dismantled. The concerts were unprecedented gestures of cooperation, the musicians representing former East Germany, West Germany, and the four powers that had partitioned Berlin after World War II. Bernstein supported Amnesty International from its inception. To benefit the effort in 1987, he established the Felicia Montealegre Fund in memory of his wife who died in 1978. In 1990, Bernstein received the Praemium Imperiale, an international prize created in 1988 by the Japan Arts Association and awarded for lifetime achievement in the arts. Bernstein used the $100,000 prize to establish The Bernstein Education Through the Arts (BETA) Fund, Inc. before his death on October 14, 1990.

Bernstein was the father of three children—Jamie, Alexander, and Nina— and the grandfather of two: Francisca and Evan.

Vienna, 1984

of the Bernstein Education Through the Arts Fund and founding chairman of the Leonard Bernstein Center for Education Through the Arts.
(pages 4/5 and 10/11)

Schuyler Chapin

First professional contacts between Bernstein and Chapin in 1959 led over the years to the growth of a close personal friendship, which Mr. Chapin describes in his book *Leonard Bernstein— Notes from a Friend*, published in 1992. Chapin, now the Commissioner of Cultural Affairs for the City of New York, is a board member of the Bernstein Education Through the Arts Fund.
(pages 144/145)

Betty Comden

In more than 50 years of collaboration, the actors, dancers and writers Betty Comden and Adolph Green have written scripts and texts for some of the most famous and beloved Broadway musicals and Hollywood films ever produced, including *Singin' in the Rain* and, for Leonard Bernstein, *On the Town* and *Wonderful Town*.
(pages 62/63)

Stanley Donen

Awarded a Lifetime Achievement Oscar in 1998, Stanley Donen, director and producer of such films as *Singin' in the Rain, Indiscreet* and *Charade*, directed with Gene Kelly Bernstein's musical *On the Town* in 1949.
(page 126)

Christoph Eschenbach

The internationally renowned and sought-after pianist and conductor, most recently head conductor of the Houston Symphony Orchestra, assumed the post of director of the Symphony Orchestra of the North German Broadcasting System in 1999. During one of his visits to Bernstein's former apartment on New York's Park Avenue, he is said to have been sent by the doorman to the delivery entrance because of his clothing—jeans and a leather jacket. As a result of the incident, as the story goes, Bernstein's wife Felicia

Alfred Altenburger

As violinist and member of the board of directors of the Vienna Philharmonic Orchestra (1973–1993), he experienced Leonard Bernstein at numerous concerts, on tours and within the context of record and film productions. Today, Alfred Altenburger is a member of the board of directors of the Gustav Mahler Youth Orchestra, a group founded by Claudio Abbado, and, since 1999, musical director of the newly established Gustav Mahler Youth + Music Foundation in Bozen.
(pages 76/77)

Hildegard Behrens

Hildegard Behrens did not begin studying voice until after completion of her final examination in law. Following a few brief years as a novice, the soprano achieved her breakthrough when Herbert von Karajan invited her to sing the part of Salome at the Salzburg Festival in 1977. Since then, she has appeared as a guest performer at nearly all of the world's major opera houses. Luciano Berio composed *Cronaca del Luogo* for her, an opera that premiered at the Salzburg Festival in 1999.
(pages 18/19 and 24/25)

Alexander Bernstein

Leonard Bernstein's son Alexander, who has supported this book project from the very beginning, is President

decided to move from the East to the West Side.
(pages 48/49)

August Everding (1928–1999)

August Everding is regarded as one of the last great figures of the theater world. After twenty years as stage director and director general of the Munich Chamber Theater, he devoted himself almost exclusively to music theater (while serving as director general in Hamburg and Munich, he directed performances at many of the world's great opera houses), while involving himself increasingly in the field of cultural policy from his adopted home in Munich beginning in the mid-1980s. Like Everding, Bernstein also sought to shake an audience asleep with its eyes open out of its slumber.
(pages 30–33)

Domiziana Giordano

A native of Rome, the actress has played leading roles in films by Tarkowskij, Roeg and Godard, to name only a few. She now works primarily as a video artist and photographer. In the late 1990s her installations have been exhibited primarily in Milan and Rome.
(pages 38/39)

Ivry Gitlis

Now a resident of Paris, the Israeli violinist—a cult figure among his peers— gave his debut in London in the mid-1940s. Since then, he has enjoyed great critical and popular success during a career that has taken him around the globe. Truffaut and Schlöndorff are by no means the only directors who have taken advantage of his passion for the cinema to engage Gitlis as a composer and performer. His autobiography *L'Âme et la Corde* was published in 1981.
(pages 148/149)

Adolph Green

In more than 50 years of collaboration, the actors, dancers and writers Betty Comden and Adolph Green have written scripts and texts for some of the most famous and beloved Broadway musicals and Hollywood films ever produced,
including *Singin' in the Rain* and, for Leonard Bernstein, *On the Town* and *Wonderful Town.*
(pages 114/115)

Thomas Hampson

The versatile American baritone has long since joined the elite among the world's opera and *Lieder* singers. In addition to the "classical" repertoire, he has also compiled and studied works from the multifaceted history of American music. He recorded Bernstein's musical *Wonderful Town* under the direction of Simon Rattle in 1998 and is eager to have other Bernstein compositions recorded.
(pages 16/17)

Charlie Harmon

Charlie Harmon studied composition at the Carnegie-Mellon University. He was hired as Leonard Bernstein's personal assistant in 1982. In 1985 he became Bernstein's archivist and was later appointed as his music editor. Harmon has been working on a critical edition of Leonard Bernstein's compositions since 1990.
(pages 28/29)

Margot Hielscher

The versatile actress and singer made her film debut alongside Zarah Leander in *Das Herz der Königin* in 1939. In course of the following decades she has played leading roles in over 50 films and appeared in countless radio and television productions. During those years she has often returned to the stage, even taking roles in boulevard theater, and has—fortunately—not even begun to think about retiring.
(pages 96/97)

Horant H. Hohlfeld

Over the course of his more than thirty years as a producer and director for the film company UNITEL, he has been closely involved in the realization of over 300 musical productions featuring virtually all of the most prominent conductors, directors and soloists. His films, particularly his documentaries and concert films with Leonard Bernstein, have earned him considerable international acclaim.
(pages 72/73)

Harry J. Kraut

Anyone who wanted to see Leonard Bernstein had to get past Harry Kraut. The Harvard graduate became his friend's manager and producer as well as the Executive Vice-President of Bernstein's company Amberson, Inc., in 1971. After Bernstein's death, he was appointed executor, trustee and general manager of the Bernstein estate. Mr. Kraut has also served as President of the Arts, Planning and Design Company, a worldwide cultural consulting firm, since 1987.
(pages 70/71)

Robert Lantz

The legendary New York agent and head of The Lantz Office enjoyed a long and close friendship with Leonard Bernstein and his family. He is on the board of supervisors of Amberson, Inc., the Bernstein company in New York, and acted as Bernstein's literary agent for several decades.
(pages 50/51)

Chester Ludgin

The American baritone, whose career began in a nightclub many years ago, was engaged by Leonard Bernstein to play a leading role (Old Sam) at the premier performance of Bernstein's opera *A Quiet Place* in Houston. He later sang the role on other occasions, including the performance at the Vienna State Opera conducted by Leonard Bernstein.
(pages 64/65)

Christa Ludwig

One of Bernstein's favorite singers, the mezzo-soprano Christa Ludwig has sung in a number of Bernstein's concerts, recording projects and performances of his own works, including the production of *Candide* he conducted in London in 1989. Christa Ludwig bade farewell to the stage in 1994, bringing her long international career to a close.
(pages 46/47)

Yehudi Menuhin (1916–1999)

A native of the US, the legendary violinist, like Bernstein himself, came from a family of Russian-Jewish immigrants. He embarked upon his international concert career at the tender age of seven. Near the midpoint of his life he discovered that playing the violin was no longer enough for him, and he became a conductor. Like Bernstein, Menuhin had a special place in his heart for the musical education of children and youth. He believed firmly in the humanitarian power of music to reconcile and enlighten.
(page 8)

Lia Montoya-Palmen

The Colombian soprano has performed at the great concert halls and opera houses of Europe and South America. She has been an instructor at the Rhine Music School in Cologne since 1976.
(pages 140/141)

Judith Pisar

An American in Paris and a French woman in New York with a passionate devotion to music and contemporary art. In the early 1960s she founded The Composer Speaks—a lecture and concert bureau for composers—and succeeded in persuading Leonard Bernstein to chair the board of this institution. From 1978 to 1994 she directed the American Center in Paris, Europe's first "America House." In 1986 she organized a tribute to Leonard Bernstein, who in turn gave a concert with the London Symphony Orchestra in honor of the American Center in 1988. Judith Pisar established Arts France–USA in 1996, an organization dedicated to honoring the work of American and French composers and performing artists.
(pages 134/135)

Marcel Prawy

Prawy worked as a journalist and a music writer before joining the Vienna People's Opera as drama director in 1955, at which time he also became a professor at the Vienna School of Music and received an appointment

as an instructor at the university in Vienna. Drawing from his experience in the US, Prawy not only introduced the musical as a theatrical genre at the Volksoper but also provided brilliant translations of American works. A well-known figure, thanks to his television shows, and an esteemed opera expert, Marcel Prawy is a Viennese institution in his own right, a man respected by all artists.
(pages 68/69)

Isaac Stern

Isaac Stern is regarded as one of the greatest violinist in the world. He is one of the most widely traveled musicians of the post-war period, and he soon learned to see himself as an ambassador. During the Cold War he made a concert tour through the Soviet Union and subsequently visited the People's Republic of China. The Oscar-winning film *From Mao to Mozart* was shot during that trip. Stern is credited with preventing the demolition of Carnegie Hall in 1960 through his commitment to its preservation. He has served as President of the Carnegie Hall Corporation since 1962. Incidentally, the close friends Stern and Bernstein celebrated their Carnegie Hall debuts in the same year (1943).
(page 146)

Mark Stringer

The young American conductor was still a student at New York's Julliard School when he attracted Leonard Bernstein's attention. Bernstein engaged him as one of his assistants and invited him to share the baton with him on two European concert tours. Mark Stringer settled in Europe after Bernstein's death. Following five years as orchestra director at the Municipal Theater in Bern, he has become a very popular guest conductor, especially in (northern) Europe.
(pages 136/137)

Michael Tilson Thomas

The American conductor is one of the best and most versatile representatives of the younger generation. After seven years as the head conductor of the London Symphony Orchestra, he took over the San Francisco Symphony Orchestra in 1995 and has since been instrumental in the symphony's successful campaign to re-establish its international standing.
(page 133)

Craig Urquhart

Well-known primarily in the US on the basis of radio, television and record productions, the composer was Bernstein's assistant from 1985 until his death. He is still Vice-President of Public Relations for the Estate of Leonard Bernstein and Managing Editor of the Bernstein newsletter *prelude, fugue & riffs*.
(pages 104/105)

François Valéry

During the course of his life, François, the son of author Paul Valéry, held a number of high positions in the French diplomacy, serving as France's ambassador to the OECD and UNESCO, to mention only two of his posts. Aside from these activities, he was also President of the Écoles d'Arts Américaines de Fontainebleau.
(pages 130/131)

Stephen Wadsworth

The director, librettist and translator collaborated with Leonard Bernstein in writing the libretto for Bernstein's opera *A Quiet Place*, which premiered in its first version in Houston in 1983. Wadsworth directed the performances of the revised version at the Scala in Milan and the Vienna State Opera.
(pages 92/93)

Michael Wager

The film and theater actor performed under Bernstein as a speaker in Stravinsky's *Oedipus Rex* and in worldwide performances of Bernstein's Third Symphony *Kaddish*.
(pages 150/151)

Peter Weiser

Secretary General of the Vienna Concert Hall Society for many years and Vienna City Commissioner for Special Cultural Projects, Weiser translated Bernstein's books *Norton Lectures* and *Findings* into German.
(page 132)

Friedemann Winklhofer

Widely acclaimed in Europe and the US, the organist and cembalist Winklhofer performed at Bernstein's express request for recording sessions and television productions in 1988 and 1990. He also played at numerous concerts under Bernstein with the symphony orchestra of the Bavarian Radio. Friedemann Winklhofer is a professor at the Munich Conservatory.
(page 52)

Martin Wöhr

Currently the director of the Studio Production and Operations Department for the radio division of the Bavarian Broadcasting Corporation, Wöhr was formerly responsible in his capacity as a sound engineer for musical productions, particularly for recordings of the symphony orchestra of the Bavarian Radio, including a number featuring Leonard Bernstein as conductor.
(pages 26/27)

Krystian Zimerman

The Polish pianist has already gained acclaim as one of today's outstanding musicians, and not only of his own generation. Aside from his patron Arthur Rubinstein, the conductors Carlo Maria Giulini, Herbert von Karajan and Leonard Bernstein have been among the most important musical figures in his life.
(pages 86/87)

Thomas R. Seiler was born in Munich on December 30, 1958. He studied history of art, literature, and drama in Munich and Paris and graduated from the Sorbonne with a master's thesis about Henri Cartier-Bresson. He then participated in a film workshop at New York University (NYU). He is a self-taught photographer and currently lives as an art historian and freelance photographer in Paris and Munich. His aim is to reveal in his photos—without the least hint of voyeurism—the personal, human sides of his subjects, aspects often hidden from view in "official" portraits.

Thomas R. Seiler met Bernstein in early 1981 at a dress rehearsal party in Munich. The conductor was so impressed with Seiler's subsequent photographs that he offered him the chance to accompany him as unofficial photographer alongside his studies.

My sincerest thanks are due to all who lent their support for the realization of this book.
I am especially grateful to the friends and acquaintances of Leonard Bernstein who readily agreed to complement my photographs with their remembrances.

Imprint

Translations from the German:
    Julian Cooper, John S. Southard and Melissa Thorson-Hause
Project coordinator:
    Robert Züblin
Editorial direction:
    Sara Schindler and Mirjam Ghisleni-Stemmle
Art direction, Design, Typography:
    Atelier Markus Bruggisser, Zurich, collaboration: Lucia Frey, Wild & Frey, Zurich
Enlargements of black-and-white negatives:
    blow up, Munich and Küffer & Stämmler, Munich
Lithography:
    Alpha Druckereiservice GmbH, Radolfzell, Germany
Printing:
    Spefa Druck AG, Zurich
Binding:
    Buchbinderei Burkhardt AG, Mönchaltorf, Switzerland

ISBN 3-908161-98-3